TICKET TO TI

SUPER BOWL

MARTIN GITLIN

ADMIT ONE

THE BIG GAME

YOUR FRONT ROW SEAT

45th Parallel Press

Published in the United States of America by Cherry Lake Publishing Group
Ann Arbor, Michigan
www.cherrylakepublishing.com

Reading Adviser: Beth Walker Gambro, MS Ed., Reading Consultant, Yorkville, IL
Book Designer: Jen Wahi

Photo Credits: Cover: © Sports Images/Dreamstime.com; page 5: © Jerry Coli/Dreamstime.com; page 7: © Arturo Holmes/Shutterstock; page 9: © Jerry Coli/Dreamstime.com; page 11: © Jerry Coli/Dreamstime.com; page 12: © Jerry Coli/Dreamstime.com; page 15: © Jerry Coli/Dreamstime.com; page 16: © Jerry Coli/Dreamstime.com; page 17: © Jerry Coli/Dreamstime.com; page 19: © Jerry Coli/Dreamstime.com; page 23: © Jerry Coli/Dreamstime.com; page 24: © Steve Jacobson/Shutterstock; page 27: © Jerry Coli/Dreamstime.com

45th Parallel Press is an imprint of Cherry Lake Publishing Group.

Library of Congress Cataloging-in-Publication Data

Names: Gitlin, Martin, author.
Title: Ticket to the Super Bowl / Martin Gitlin.
Description: Ann Arbor, Michigan : Cherry Lake Publishing, [2023] | Series: The big game | Audience: Grades 4-6 | Summary: "Who has won the Super Bowl? Who were the most valuable players? Written as high interest with struggling readers in mind, this series includes considerate vocabulary, engaging content and fascinating facts, clear text and formatting, and compelling photos. Educational sidebars include extra fun facts and information about each game. Includes table of contents, glossary, index, and author biography"-- Provided by publisher.
Identifiers: LCCN 2022039945 | ISBN 9781668919545 (hardcover) | ISBN 9781668920565 (paperback) | ISBN 9781668921890 (ebook) | ISBN 9781668923221 (pdf)
Subjects: LCSH: Super Bowl--History--Juvenile literature. | National Football League--History--Juvenile literature. | Football--United States--History--Juvenile literature. | Football--Miscellanea--Juvenile literature.
Classification: LCC GV956.2.S8 G58 2023 | DDC 796.332/648--dc23/eng/20220901
LC record available at https://lccn.loc.gov/2022039945

Cherry Lake Publishing would like to acknowledge the work of the Partnership for 21st Century Learning, a network of Battelle for Kids. Please visit http://www.battelleforkids.org/networks/p21

Printed in the United States of America
Corporate Graphics

Table of Contents

Introduction

It is not just a football game. It is an event. It is the most popular sports contest in America.

It is the Super Bowl. The battle is for the National Football League (NFL) title. It draws more viewers than any TV show every year.

The NFL has 32 teams. They play in conferences. This is how teams are organized. They are divided into 2 conferences. One is the American Football Conference (AFC). The other is the National Football Conference (NFC).

The season begins in early September. Each team plays 17 games.

Winners raise the Vince Lombardi Trophy in the air. Each team that wins a Super Bowl gets their own trophy to keep.

The NFL gets more exciting after the regular season. That is when the playoffs begin. The teams with the best records play. The winners advance to the next round. The playoffs continue until 2 teams remain. They are the winners of the AFC and NFC.

Those 2 teams meet in the Super Bowl. It is played 2 weeks after the playoffs end. More than 100 million people watch the game each year.

Tom Brady talks to his team during one of his 6 Super Bowl championship games with the New England Patriots. Brady holds the record for most Super Bowl wins for an NFL player.

Super Game, Super History

In the 1960s, NFL teams didn't just play on the field. Off the field, they competed to sign the best players.

That was because there was another league. It was the American Football League. The AFL began in 1960. Its teams tried to attract talent from the NFL.

Then came June 8, 1966. That day, the 2 leagues agreed to merge. That means they formed one league. They did not complete the merger until 1970. But they made a plan in 1967. They planned for their champion teams to play each other.

The big game needed a name. It was at first known only as the "World Championship." How it became the Super Bowl is not certain.

The Green Bay Packers won the first 2 Super Bowls.

One story credits Kansas City Chiefs owner Lamar Hunt. He was watching his kids play with a toy called a Super Ball. The toy gave Hunt an idea. He decided to name the AFL–NFL clash the Super Bowl.

Some say that story isn't true. But the game has sure been a success.

The NFL Green Bay Packers won the first 2 Super Bowls easily. Many fans believed the NFL was better than the AFL.

The AFL Jets wanted to prove them wrong. They did in 1969. They pulled perhaps the biggest upset in Super Bowl history. They were supposed to lose badly to Baltimore. But they beat the Colts.

The Miami Dolphins made history in 1972. They did not lose a game all year. They became the only Super Bowl winner in history with a perfect season.

In the 1970s, a terrible team became great. That was Pittsburgh. The Steelers struggled in the 1960s. But they built an amazing defense. They won 4 Super Bowls from 1975 to 1980.

Quarterback Aaron Rodgers gets ready to throw the ball toward the end zone for a touchdown! This is called a touchdown pass.

San Francisco was the team of the 1980s. Quarterback Joe Montana led the way. Montana threw touchdowns to Jerry Rice. Many believe Rice is the greatest receiver ever. Receivers catch the football. Montana and Rice helped the 49ers win 4 Super Bowls in 9 years.

Buffalo never won a Super Bowl through 2022. But the Bills did what no other team has done. They earned 4 straight trips to the big game. They lost every Super Bowl from 1991 to 1994.

The Bills were not the only unhappy team. Denver lost 3 Super Bowls from 1987 to 1990. But Broncos quarterback John Elway changed that. He became a Hall of Fame player. And his team earned titles in 1998 and 1999.

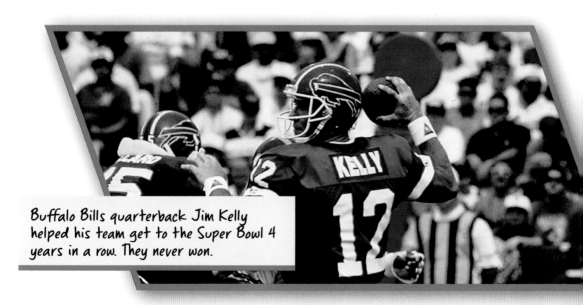

Buffalo Bills quarterback Jim Kelly helped his team get to the Super Bowl 4 years in a row. They never won.

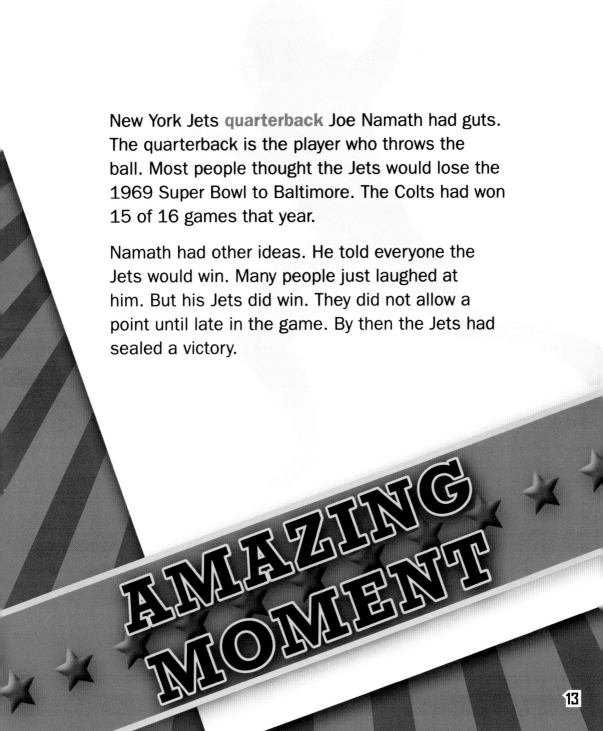

New York Jets **quarterback** Joe Namath had guts. The quarterback is the player who throws the ball. Most people thought the Jets would lose the 1969 Super Bowl to Baltimore. The Colts had won 15 of 16 games that year.

Namath had other ideas. He told everyone the Jets would win. Many people just laughed at him. But his Jets did win. They did not allow a point until late in the game. By then the Jets had sealed a victory.

AMAZING MOMENT

The Early Heroes

Superstars often played super in Super Bowls. But sometimes heroes came out of nowhere.

The first was a good player. But he was no superstar. He was Green Bay receiver Max McGee. McGee was at the end of his career in 1967. But he came through in the first Super Bowl. He caught 7 passes for 138 yards. And he scored 2 touchdowns.

Quarterbacks are the biggest football stars. But sometimes players on defense stand out.

Randy White of the Dallas Cowboys on his way in for a tackle. De-fense! De-fense!

Among them were Harvey Martin and Randy White. They were Dallas linemen. Linemen work to tackle players with the ball. Martin and White combined for 3 sacks in the 1978 Super Bowl. Sacks are when quarterbacks are tackled for negative yards. Their team easily beat Denver.

It was also no wonder Washington beat Miami in 1982. That is because fullback John Riggins ran wild. He ran for 166 yards in that game. He even scored a 43-yard touchdown.

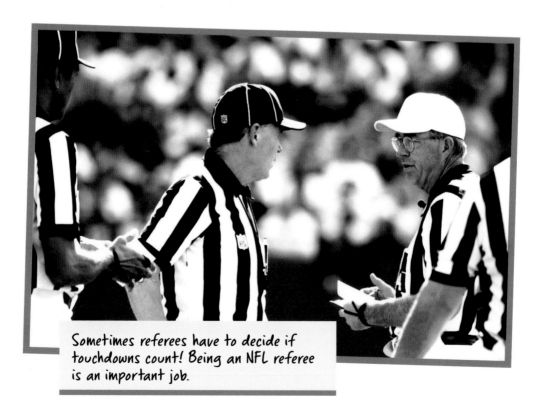

Sometimes referees have to decide if touchdowns count! Being an NFL referee is an important job.

Washington's John Riggins fights his way down the field.

Super San Francisco

Perhaps the greatest title game ever was played by Jerry Rice. The San Francisco receiver was amazing in 1989.

Rice could not be stopped against Cincinnati. He caught 11 passes for an amazing 215 yards. That remains a Super Bowl record. He also scored a touchdown.

That effort might have gone to waste. But the 49ers came through in the fourth quarter. Quarterback Joe Montana tossed a touchdown pass to win it.

Montana was not the only 49ers quarterback to shine. He was replaced after he retired by Steve Young. Young set a Super Bowl mark in 1995. That is when he fired 6 touchdown passes. His team wiped out San Diego in that win.

San Francisco receiver Jerry Rice gets ready for the ball. Receivers need to keep cool under pressure to make important catches.

Montana was not the best quarterback in Super Bowl history. Tom Brady was. And he continued to be into the early 2020s.

Brady was not a star player in college. Every team passed on their chance to draft him. They did not pick him to play for their team out of college. But he became a star with New England. He led his Patriots to an amazing 9 Super Bowls. And they won 6 of them.

He was not done. Brady joined Tampa Bay in 2021. He was 43 years old. And he guided that team to a Super Bowl victory.

A few champion teams have played in more than one city. One was the Colts. The Baltimore Colts won the big game in 1971. The team moved to Indianapolis in 1984. The Indianapolis Colts won the crown in 2007.

The Rams also won Super Bowls for 2 different cities. The St. Louis Rams won it in 2000. They moved to Los Angeles in 2016. And they took the title there in 2022.

The Raiders won Super Bowls for Oakland and Los Angeles. That team moved back and forth a few times.

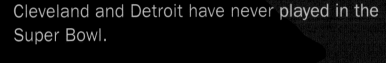

Cleveland and Detroit have never played in the Super Bowl.

The Detroit Lions have not appeared in an NFL championship game since 1957.

Browns fans have gotten their hopes up and been let down more often. Their team played in AFL or AFC title games 5 times. And they lost them all.

WAY BACK WHEN

The Later Years

Another quarterback shined for St. Louis in 2000. His name was Kurt Warner. He set a Super Bowl record that year. He passed for 414 yards to beat Tennessee. Most amazing is that he did not throw an interception. That is when the opposing team catches a pass.

The best player in 2014 was not a quarterback. It was Seattle linebacker Malcolm Smith. Linebackers play defense. Smith took over the Super Bowl. He intercepted a pass with his team leading 15–0. Then he ran it back for a touchdown.

Smith also recovered a fumble. That is when the ball falls to the ground. Smith had 9 tackles. His play helped the Seahawks beat Denver 43–8.

St. Louis Rams quarterback Kurt Warner searches for an opening before his pass.

Tampa quarterback Tom Brady works to pump up the crowd. He does this before every game.

The 2022 Super Bowl had many stars. Among them was Rams receiver Cooper Kupp. He was the best receiver in the NFL all season. And he stood out against Cincinnati.

Kupp caught 8 passes for 92 yards. He also scored 2 touchdowns. His skill played a big role in the victory. It also stopped Cincinnati from winning its first Super Bowl.

- ☆ Super quarterback Tom Brady played in 10 Super Bowls. He owns many Super Bowl records. One of them is total passing yards. He threw for 3,039 yards through 2022.

- ☆ Brady set a Super Bowl mark in 2018. That is when he threw for 505 yards. He also tossed 3 touchdown passes. But it was not enough. His Patriots lost that game to the Eagles.

- ☆ Brady even led the greatest Super Bowl comeback ever. New England trailed Atlanta by 25 points in 2017. But New England was not done. Brady guided them to 3 touchdowns in the second half. He then led a touchdown drive to win it.

LEGENDS OF THE SPORT

Fantastic Finishes

There have been many Super Bowl heroes. There have also been some who failed in big moments. Among them was Buffalo **placekicker** Scott Norwood.

It was 1991. The Giants were battling the Bills. Buffalo back Thurman Thomas had rushed for 135 yards. He helped his team drive downfield.

Norwood would decide victory or defeat. He lined up to kick a 47-yard **field goal**. He booted it far enough. But it floated to the right. The Bills had lost their first Super Bowl. They also lost the next 3.

The 2000 Super Bowl was one of the most exciting ever. It had an incredible finish. Tennessee scored a field goal with 2 minutes left. The Titans and the Rams were tied.

Former Buffalo Bills running back Thurman Thomas searches for an opening to move the ball down the field.

St. Louis quarterback Kurt Warner went to work. He marched his team downfield. He tossed a touchdown pass to Isaac Bruce. That put his team ahead.

The Titans were not done. They drove to within 10 yards of the winning score. Quarterback Steve McNair threw a pass. Receiver Kevin Dyson caught it. He raced toward the goal line.

That is when Rams linebacker Mike Jones played hero. He stopped Dyson a foot short of a touchdown. Time ran out. St. Louis had won its first Super Bowl.

The 2008 Super Bowl was also a thriller. New England was trying to finish its season 19–0. No team had been unbeaten since the 1972 Dolphins. But the Giants hoped to stop them.

The Giants had stopped Patriots quarterback Tom Brady. They stayed in the game. Giants quarterback Eli Manning threw a pass to David Tyree. Tyree made perhaps the greatest catch in Super Bowl history. He pinned the ball against his helmet and snagged it.

That set up the winning touchdown. Manning fired a pass to Plaxico Burress that sealed victory. It was not easy beating Tom Brady. But Manning had done it. It was perhaps the biggest upset in NFL history.

★ The Pittsburgh Steelers and the New England Patriots have won the most Super Bowls. They both won 6!

★ The San Francisco 49ers and the Dallas Cowboys are next with 5 Super Bowl wins each.

★ The Minnesota Vikings and the Buffalo Bills have both played in the Super Bowl 4 times. They've never won!

★ Four teams have never played in a Super Bowl: the Cleveland Browns, the Detroit Lions, the Jacksonville Jaguars, and the Houston Texans.

! A BIT OF TRIVIA

Activity

Go online and read about your favorite football team. Learn about a player who had a tough time as a child. Find out all he had to overcome to star in the NFL. Then ask your teacher if you can write about him.

Learn More

BOOKS

Holloway, Jerrett. *Football for Kids: Learn the Basics and Play the Game*. Emeryville, CA: Rockridge Press, 2021. Paragon Publishing.

Football's Greatest Games for Kids: The 20 Greatest Games That Every Football Fan Must Know. Independently published, 2022.

Wetzel, Dan. *Epic Athletes: Tom Brady*. New York: Henry Holt and Company, 2019.

WEBSITES

NFL Play 60: https://www.nfl.com/causes/play60/

Sports Illustrated Kids: Football: https://www.sikids.com/football

DLTK's Site for Kids: Super Bowl Sunday: https://www.dltk-kids.com/sports/superbowl.htm

Glossary

conferences (KAHN-fuh-ruhn-sez) two groups of teams into which the NFL is divided

draft (DRAFT) event in which NFL teams pick the best college players to join them

field goal (FEELD GOHL) 3-point kick through the uprights

fumble (FUHM-buhl) dropped ball that can be recovered by either team

interception (in-tuhr-SEP-shuhn) pass caught by the defensive team

linebacker (LYN-bah-kuhr) position on defense between the linemen and defensive backs

linemen (LYN-mehn) players who have the front position on defense

merge (MERJ) to combine

placekicker (PLAYS-kik-uhr) player who kicks field goals and extra points

playoffs (PLAY-awfs) series of games that determine the Super Bowl teams

quarterback (KWOR-tuhr-bak) player mostly responsible for throwing passes

receiver (rih-SEE-vuhr) player mostly responsible for catching passes

sacks (SAKS) tackling of the quarterback behind the line of scrimmage

upset (UHP-set) unexpected win by a team

Index

About the Author

Marty Gitlin is a sports book author based in Cleveland. He won more than 45 awards as a newspaper sportswriter from 1991 to 2002. Included was a first-place award from the Associated Press for his coverage of the 1995 World Series. He has had more than 200 books published since 2006. Most of them were written for students.